Overcoming Procrastination

Stop Waiting. Start Doing

Dr. Barbara Whitehead

ISBN

Paperback: 978-1-969066-88-7

Hardcover: 978-1-969066-89-4

Published by: Columbus Book Publishers

www.columbusbookpublishers.com

Printed in the United States of America

Dedication

Thank you to my entire publishing support team for ensuring this book found its way into the hands of the readers who need it most and for the meticulous work that polished the final product.

Acknowledgment

I owe a debt of gratitude to the many individuals and organisations who supported me on this journey, especially to those who patiently endured the long, sometimes messy, and occasionally frantic process of bringing this book from a scattered idea to a finished manuscript.

About the Author

Dr. Barbara Whitehead: Spiritual Leader & Mentor Dr. Barbara Whitehead is a multifaceted entrepreneur, transformative life coach, and spiritual leader dedicated to empowering individuals to reach their divine destiny. Known for being "on the pulse of the people," she combines media influence with hands-on ministry to mentor leaders and guide youth. Key Leadership Roles & Contributions: Global Mentorship: As the Senior Consultant for the International Kingdom Coalition, she provides spiritual covering and mentorship to pastors and leaders across the globe. Youth Advocacy: She serves as the President of Confident Kids Inc., a nonprofit organization focused on teaching essential life skills to the younger generation. Ministry Coordination: Dr. Whitehead is the Coordinator of Jesus Women USA (serving through Godhead Prayer Ministry). In this role, she fosters international prayer, discipleship, and unity within the body of Christ. Media Presence: She is a well-known radio and television personality who utilizes these platforms to share her message of salvation and empowerment. Her Core Mission: To see souls saved and to empower believers to fulfill the potential they were divinely destined to achieve.

Table of Contents

Introduction...i

Chapter 1: Why Procrastination is a Problem 1

Chapter 2: Acknowledge The Problem 4

Chapter 3: Understanding The Problem....................................9

Psychological and Emotional Indicators: Playing the Mind Game! 9

Procrasti-Pattern Checklist 25

Chapter 4: Identify the Root Cause..26

Why You Procrastinate and How It Affects You 30

Checklist 30

Chapter 5: Find the Habit and Break the Cycle 33

Breaking Free from Procrastination Identifying and Overcoming

Habits Worksheet... 34

Chapter 6: You Can Change Negative Habits...........................40

Break Tasks into Smaller Steps 40

Set Deadlines 41

Use Positive Self-Talk.. 42

Minimize Distractions 43

Reward Yourself... 43

Get Support 44

The Procrastination Log/Tracker 46

Overcoming Procrastination Habits and Patterns 51

Recognizing Procrastination Habits and Patterns........................... 52

Halting Procrastination Habits and Patterns 57

9 Ways to Change Your Behavior 62

Encouragement for Procrastinators 64

Next Steps 65

Becoming More Productive and Overcoming Procrastination
Checklist 70

Becoming More Productive and Overcoming Procrastination
Worksheet 73

Is Validation Holding You Back from Success?............................. 77

Addressing the Need for Validation:.. 77

Childhood Experiences and the Need for Validation 78

How the Need for Validation Contributes to Procrastination...... 79

Cultivate Self-Validation 83

Manage External Interactions 84

Breaking Free from Procrastination... 85

Understand Your Procrastination Style 85

Make Tasks More Manageable and Appealing 86

Boost Self-Efficacy and Confidence 87

Implement Time Management and Accountability 87

Practice Self-Compassion 88

Envy and Comparison Lead to Failure 90

How Envy and Comparison Lead to Failure: 90

How Envy and Comparison Lead to Procrastination: 92

Breaking the Cycle: 93

Impacts Quality of Work 95

Overcoming Procrastination through Scriptural Mindfulness, Prayer and Meditation 95

What is Scriptural Mindfulness, Prayer and Meditation? 96

How Scriptural Mindfulness and Meditation Can Help You Overcome Procrastination? 97

Tips for Integrating Scriptural Mindfulness and Meditation into Your Routine 98

Prayer: Invoking Divine Assistance and Guidance 101

Meditation: Cultivating Inner Stillness and Focus 102

Integration for Holistic Overcoming of Procrastination 103

Bible Scriptures and Affirmations to Overcome Procrastination 104

Introduction

Hey friend! I've been thinking about you, and something's been on my mind. I've noticed a bit of a pattern lately with some things getting put off, and I just wanted to chat about how procrastination can sometimes quietly mess with our lives and even our bigger picture, like our destiny.

Procrastination is defined as the act of unnecessarily delaying or postponing tasks, decisions, or actions, despite knowing that there will likely be negative consequences for doing so. It's not simply being busy or prioritizing other things; it's a deliberate (though often irrational) delay of something that needs to be done. The word itself comes from the Latin "procrastinatus," meaning "to put off until tomorrow."

It's easy to fall into the trap of delaying things, especially when tasks feel big or tough. We all do it sometimes, but when it becomes a habit, it can start to build up. Those small delays can turn into missed opportunities.

Think about it: if you're always waiting until the last minute, you might not be putting out your best work, or you could be missing out on chances that pop up because you're tied up playing catch-up.

Beyond just the immediate stress, consistent procrastination can really impact your potential. Each time you put something off, you might be sidelining a chance to learn something new, develop a skill, or even just feel the satisfaction of ticking something off your list. Over time, that can add up and actually steer you away from where you want to go. Your "destiny" isn't some fixed thing; it's shaped by the choices you make every day. And choosing to delay can inadvertently close off paths that might have led to amazing things.

It's not about being perfect, but being mindful. Maybe it's worth thinking about what's behind the procrastination. Whatever it is, getting a handle on it can really open things up for you. I'm concerned because you are absolutely amazing, and I don't want you to miss your next move because of procrastination.

Chapter 1: Why Procrastination is a Problem

Procrastination is a significant problem because it can lead to a cascade of negative effects across various aspects of your life. Let's look at some of the issues it can cause:

Increased Stress and Anxiety: As deadlines approach and tasks remain undone, stress levels skyrocket. This can lead to feelings of overwhelm, guilt, and even panic. The constant worry about unfulfilled obligations can have a serious toll on mental well-being.

Poor Performance and Missed Opportunities: Delaying tasks often means rushing to complete them at the last minute, leading to lower-quality work. This can result in missed deadlines, poorer grades in academic settings, reduced job performance, and even lost opportunities for career advancement or personal growth.

Negative Impact on Self-Esteem and Self-Worth: Chronic procrastination can make you feel unproductive, lazy, and ineffectual. This can erode self-confidence and contribute to a negative self-image, fostering a cycle of self-defeating behavior.

Damage to Relationships: When commitments are consistently delayed or ignored, it can lead to frustration and resentment from others, whether they are colleagues, classmates, friends, or family members. This can strain relationships and erode trust.

Health Problems: The chronic stress associated with procrastination can manifest physically, leading to issues like insomnia, digestive problems, muscle tension, and a weakened immune system. Procrastinators may also delay important health check-ups or treatments.

Limited Personal Growth and Skill Development: By avoiding challenging or unpleasant tasks, procrastinators miss opportunities to learn new skills, develop resilience, and expand their capabilities. This can hinder personal and professional development.

Reduced Productivity and Efficiency: Procrastination inherently leads to a decrease in overall productivity. Time that could be spent constructively is wasted on avoidance behaviors, making it harder to achieve goals and make progress.

Financial Consequences: In some cases, procrastination can have direct financial repercussions, such as late fees on bills, missed financial opportunities, or even job loss.

In essence, while procrastination might offer a temporary escape from an unpleasant task, its long-term costs far outweigh any immediate benefits. It creates a vicious cycle of stress, underperformance, and diminished well-being. By adopting effective strategies and a proactive mindset, you can conquer procrastination and begin making progress toward your goals.

Chapter 2: Acknowledge The Problem

The first step in overcoming procrastination is recognizing and admitting that it's a problem. If you are putting off tasks until the last minute, avoiding essential duties, or feeling overwhelmed by your to-do list, you are experiencing procrastination. By acknowledging the problem, you can start taking action to address it. This is true for anything in life that you want to change—you must name it and face it before you can work on fixing it.

The most obvious sign of procrastination is delay and avoidance. It's not just being "lazy," but it's often a complex interplay of emotions, fears, and habits.

Here's an objective description of procrastination:

Repeatedly Postponing Tasks: You find yourself saying "I'll do it later," "I'll do it tomorrow," or "Now isn't a good time" for things you know you need to do. This applies to big projects, small chores, important decisions, or even responding to messages.

Struggling to Start: Even when you want to get started on a task, you feel an inexplicable resistance or inability to begin. You might sit down, open your computer, and then find yourself browsing social media or doing anything else instead.

Prioritizing Trivial Tasks: You spend time on less important or urgent activities (e.g., cleaning, organizing, endlessly checking email/social media) as a way to avoid the truly important work. This is sometimes called "productive procrastination."

Making Excuses: You constantly justify your delays with reasons like "I work better under pressure," "I need to be in the right mood," or "I don't have enough information yet."

Waiting Until the Last Minute: You consistently find yourself racing against deadlines, pulling all-nighters, or submitting work that isn't your best because you ran out of time. The rush of the deadline can sometimes feel like a motivator, but it's often a symptom of procrastination.

Postponing tasks is a super common habit, and honestly, we've all been there! It's that sneaky feeling of "I'll do it later" that often leads to stress and rushed work. But don't worry, it's a habit you can definitely tackle.

If you're consistently delaying tasks, it's not just situational. You didn't just run out of time. There are other factors to consider. Emotional and psychological factors contribute to procrastination. Emotionally, you might notice feelings of anxiety or dread when thinking about a task. This can often lead you to avoid it altogether.

You might also experience a sense of guilt or shame after procrastinating, which can then feed into a cycle of more avoidance.

Psychologically, it often stems from perfectionism (fear of not doing something perfectly), a fear of failure, or even a fear of success. You might find yourself easily distracted by less important things, rationalizing why you can't start the task, or feeling overwhelmed by the sheer size of the project. If you're noticing these feelings, it's a good sign to dig a little deeper into why you're putting things off!

Are you brave enough to consider why you postpone doing what needs to be done when it needs to be done? Each person's pattern is unique, and the reasons are personal.

It helps to understand why we put things off. Ask yourself which factor is contributing to your experience. Does the task feel so overwhelming that you don't even know where to start? Are you afraid of failing or even succeeding? Perhaps you feel stuck because you are comparing your results to someone else's results. And let's be real, sometimes tasks are just plain boring!

No one likes to feel stressed and anxious. As deadlines loom, procrastination begins causing an increase in anxiety and stress. You might find yourself caught in the loop of putting things off and experiencing an ever-present undercurrent of anxiety. You might also feel a constant underlying worry about tasks you haven't started or completed.

Overcoming Procrastination

The guilt of avoiding tasks you know you should be doing can fuel a cycle of procrastination and harsh self-criticism, leading to lower self-esteem and feelings of Impostor Syndrome. Over time, this struggle can feel like a never-ending battle.

You might start to resent tasks you once found manageable or even enjoyable. It feels like things are piling up, and resentment is building up. This resentment can spill over into other areas of your daily life.

Pay attention. Are you engaging in harsh self-criticism or have an inner voice that tells you "you're not good enough" or "you'll never succeed?" Negative self-talk is an important indicator that must be recognized as a problem. It is essential to know yourself. It is also imperative to recognize when there is a problem. Finally, you have to address the issue.

I mentioned fear of success earlier as a probable cause of procrastination. It's less common, but some people procrastinate because they fear the implications of success, which may or may not bring additional responsibilities, and consequently, more stress.

Another main culprit of procrastination is losing focus and finding it difficult to concentrate. Are you easily distracted? When you're procrastinating, it can be hard to focus on the task at hand. You might find yourself easily sidetracked by notifications, irrelevant thoughts, or external stimuli.

Do you ever find yourself putting things off, even when you know it's probably not the best idea? Of course, we all do it sometimes, but if it's a regular thing, there might be some deeper stuff going on. Are you willing to acknowledge the problem?

The questions I have mentioned in this chapter are important for identifying your behavior and thinking patterns, as well as the triggers that can lead to procrastination.

Chapter 3: Understanding The Problem

Procrastination might not seem like it in some cases, but it can be more of a problem than we realize.

Psychological and Emotional Indicators: Playing the Mind Game!

1. Perfectionism

This one's a biggie! Sometimes we put things off because we're so worried about not doing it absolutely perfectly. It's like, "If I can't do it flawlessly, why start at all?" This fear of not meeting super-high standards can paralyze us.

Perfectionism often starts from a mix of personality traits and life experiences. Some people grow up in environments where mistakes weren't tolerated, leading them to tie their self-worth to flawless performance. Others might be naturally wired to strive for excellence, feeling a deep need to meet impossibly high standards. While aiming for high-quality work isn't necessarily a bad thing, perfectionism can quickly become a productivity killer.

9

Instead of just getting things done, perfectionists can get stuck overthinking, tweaking tiny details, and delaying tasks because they fear making mistakes. This can lead to procrastination, burnout, and a constant feeling that nothing is ever good enough.

2. Fear of Failure (or even success!)

Yep, both ends of the spectrum can be equally detrimental. We might delay a task because we're scared of messing up, getting judged, or not being good enough. But sometimes, it's also a fear of success! Success can bring new responsibilities or expectations, which can be daunting.

Fear of failure is one of the biggest drivers of procrastination. When people worry that they won't succeed or that their work won't be good enough, they often delay starting tasks to avoid facing that anxiety. Instead of tackling the challenge head-on, they put it off, hoping to sidestep the discomfort. But the longer they wait, the more overwhelming the task feels, creating a vicious cycle of avoidance and stress.

Psychologists explain that procrastination can be a form of self-protection—if you don't start, you can't fail, right? Unfortunately, this mindset only makes things worse. The fear grows, deadlines loom, and the pressure intensifies, leading to rushed work, missed opportunities, and even lower confidence. Over time, this pattern can reinforce negative beliefs about one's abilities, making it even harder to break free from procrastination.

Fear of success might sound counterintuitive, but it can be a sneaky reason people procrastinate. When someone associates success with added pressure, higher expectations, or even unwanted attention, they may subconsciously delay tasks to avoid those outcomes. For example, if achieving a goal means taking on more responsibility or stepping into the spotlight, a person might hesitate, fearing they won't be able to maintain their success or that others will judge them more harshly.

This fear can lead to self-sabotage—putting off important work, missing deadlines, or not fully committing to opportunities. Some people worry that success will change their relationships or bring new challenges they're not ready for, so they procrastinate as a way to stay in their comfort zone. Over time, this pattern can reinforce negative beliefs, making it even harder to break free from avoidance.

3. Overwhelm

When a task feels massive and daunting, it seems easier to just shut down and put it off. It's like looking at a mountain and thinking, "There's no way I can climb that!"

Feeling overwhelmed can make even the simplest tasks seem impossible, leading to procrastination as a way to cope. When there's too much to do or a task feels too complex, the brain can go into shutdown mode, making it hard to figure out where to start. Instead of tackling the work, people often delay it, hoping they'll feel more prepared later—but that rarely happens. The longer they wait, the more stressful the task becomes, creating a cycle of avoidance and anxiety.

Overwhelm can also trigger decision fatigue, where making choices feels exhausting, leading to hesitation and inaction. The pressure to do everything perfectly or meet high expectations can add to the stress, making procrastination feel like a temporary relief. Unfortunately, this only makes things worse, as deadlines pile up and the weight of unfinished tasks grows heavier.

4. Lack of Clarity/Motivation

If you're unsure why you're doing something, or if it just feels boring and pointless, your brain is probably going to try and find something more interesting to do. We tend to procrastinate on tasks we don't enjoy or don't see the value in.

Lack of clarity and lack of motivation can seriously drag down productivity, making even simple tasks feel overwhelming. When people don't have a clear understanding of their goals, expectations, or next steps, they waste time second-guessing themselves, redoing work, or waiting for direction. This uncertainty can lead to frustration, hesitation, and a general slowdown in progress.

On the other hand, a lack of motivation makes it hard to stay focused and engaged. When people don't feel inspired or connected to their work, they tend to procrastinate, put in minimal effort, or struggle to push through challenges. Low motivation can also lead to higher absenteeism, poor-quality work, and a negative team atmosphere.

The combination of unclear direction and low motivation creates a cycle where productivity suffers, deadlines slip, and overall morale declines.

5. Difficulty with Self-Regulation/Impulsivity

This is about controlling your urges. If you find yourself constantly reaching for your phone, checking social media, or doing anything but the task at hand, it might be a sign that you're struggling to regulate your impulses and prioritize long-term goals over immediate gratification.

Struggling with self-regulation can make it tough to stay focused and productive, especially when impulsivity gets in the way. When someone has trouble managing their emotions, thoughts, or behaviors, they might find themselves jumping from one task to another, getting distracted easily, or making rushed decisions without thinking things through.

Impulsivity can lead to procrastination, missed deadlines, and inconsistent work quality because instead of sticking to a plan, people might act on immediate urges—whether it's scrolling social media, starting a new project before finishing the last one, or reacting emotionally to challenges. Over time, this cycle can create frustration and stress, making it even harder to stay on track. The key to improving productivity is building habits that support focus and discipline, like setting clear goals, using structured routines, and practicing mindfulness to stay present and intentional with tasks.

6. *Negative Self-Talk*

Do you find yourself thinking things like, "I'm not good enough," or "I'll never get this done?" These negative thoughts can be a huge roadblock and contribute to putting things off. Negative self-talk can seriously hold you back when it comes to productivity. When your inner voice constantly criticizes, doubts, or undermines your abilities, it creates a mental barrier that makes it harder to take action. Instead of focusing on progress, you get stuck in a cycle of self-doubt, second-guessing every decision, and fearing failure. This can lead to procrastination, lower confidence, and even burnout.

One major reason negative self-talk is so damaging is that it reinforces limiting beliefs. If you keep telling yourself, "I'm not good enough" or "I'll never get this right," your brain starts to believe it, making it harder to push through challenges. It also increases stress and anxiety, which can drain your energy and make even simple tasks feel overwhelming. Over time, this can lead to avoidance behaviors, where you delay important work because you're afraid of not meeting unrealistic expectations.

7. Distractibility

If your mind is constantly wandering, or you're easily pulled away by notifications or other things, it can be hard to buckle down and focus on what needs to be done. Getting distracted can seriously wreck your productivity because it throws off your focus and makes it harder to get things done efficiently. Every time something pulls you away—whether it's a notification, background noise, or your own wandering thoughts—it takes time to get back into the groove. In fact, studies show that after an interruption, it can take over 23 minutes to fully refocus. Now, imagine that happening multiple times a day. No wonder it feels like you're never making progress!

On top of that, distractions drain your mental energy. Constantly switching between tasks wears you out, making it harder to stay motivated and engaged. It can lead to lower-quality work, missed deadlines, and added stress. Plus, distractions often push people into multitasking mode, which might seem productive but actually makes things worse by splitting attention instead of allowing deep focus. The key to fixing this? Cut down on distractions, set boundaries, and build habits that help you stay locked in when you need to focus!

8. Chronic Lateness:

Frequently finding yourself being late for appointments, meetings, or simply getting out of the house? That's often tied to procrastination, and it can throw productivity off in a big way. A lot of times, it comes down to struggling with time management, motivation, or just underestimating how long things actually take.

Sometimes, lateness is even a form of avoidance, where people push off responsibilities or stressful situations without realizing it. Struggling to decide what to wear can even be a sneaky form of procrastination. When someone delays picking an outfit, it's often because they're overwhelmed by choices, worried about making the wrong decision, or simply avoiding the next step in their day. This hesitation can stem from decision fatigue, where too many options drain mental energy, making even simple choices feel exhausting.

For chronic procrastinators, indecision about clothing can be part of a larger pattern of delaying responsibilities. Instead of quickly choosing an outfit and moving forward, they get stuck overanalyzing, second-guessing, or even avoiding the decision altogether. This can lead to wasted time, rushed mornings, and increased stress, ultimately affecting productivity.

The effects can pile up fast—missed deadlines, rushed work, frustrated coworkers or friends. Over time, it can chip away at trust, make work relationships harder, and ramp up stress levels. Plus, it reinforces procrastination, creating even more pressure down the line. What is the best way to break the cycle? A little self-awareness, better planning, and solid time management strategies to keep things on track!

9. Unfinished Projects:

Sometimes, you might find yourself starting new projects easily and with enthusiasm, but rarely are they brought to completion. Your to-do list might contain the same items for days or weeks. Starting projects is exciting: the rush of a new idea, the motivation to dive in, the feeling that this time, you're really going to follow through. But then, life happens. Distractions pop up, motivation fades, and suddenly, that once-exciting project is collecting dust while new ideas take its place. Before you know it, your to-do list is packed with half-finished tasks that never seem to get checked off.

This pattern is a classic sign of procrastination, often fueled by perfectionism, overwhelm, or fear of failure. Sometimes, people abandon projects because they get stuck in the details, wanting everything to be just right before moving forward. Other times, the sheer size of a task feels intimidating, making it easier to push it aside for something that feels more manageable. And let's be honest, starting something new is way more fun than slogging through the messy middle of an existing project.

The problem? Unfinished projects create mental clutter, leaving you feeling frustrated and unproductive. They can also lead to a cycle of procrastination, where the guilt of not finishing makes it even harder to pick things back up.

10. Avoiding Communication

Dodging calls, ignoring emails, or putting off messages? Yep, that's procrastination in disguise. When a task feels overwhelming, stressful, or just plain annoying, avoiding communication becomes a way to delay dealing with it. Maybe it's an email about a project you haven't started, a call you know will lead to more work, or a message that requires a tough conversation—whatever it is, the longer you wait, the harder it gets to respond.

This kind of procrastination can create a snowball effect. The more you delay, the more guilt and anxiety build up, making it even tougher to face the situation. Eventually, unanswered messages pile up, deadlines slip, and relationships—whether professional or personal—start to suffer. Plus, avoiding communication can lead to missed opportunities, whether it's a job offer, an important update, or just staying connected with people who matter.

11. Impact on Relationships

Procrastination can strain relationships with colleagues, friends, and family if your delays affect others. Procrastination doesn't just mess with deadlines; it can seriously strain relationships, too.

When you constantly put off tasks, miss commitments, or delay important conversations, it can frustrate the people around you. Whether it's a coworker waiting for your part of a project, a friend wondering why you haven't responded to their message, or a family member relying on you for something, procrastination can make others feel ignored, unimportant, or even resentful.

Over time, this can erode trust. If people start seeing you as unreliable, they may hesitate to count on you, which can lead to tension and distance in relationships. It's especially tough in professional settings, where procrastination can affect teamwork and productivity. In personal relationships, it can create misunderstandings, missed opportunities, and emotional disconnects.

12. Neglecting Self-Care

Putting off important self-care activities like doctor's appointments, exercise, or healthy eating. Neglecting self-care is one of those sneaky forms of procrastination that can have a big impact on your well-being and productivity. When life gets busy, it's easy to push things like exercise, healthy eating, or even scheduling a doctor's appointment to the bottom of the to-do list. The problem? The longer you delay taking care of yourself, the harder it gets to bounce back. Eventually, it starts affecting your energy, focus, and overall performance.

Procrastinating on self-care often stems from feeling overwhelmed, prioritizing work over health, or avoiding discomfort, such as skipping a workout due to exhaustion or delaying a check-up because of the potential for bad news. But ignoring these things doesn't make them go away; it just creates more stress down the line. Poor self-care can lead to burnout, lower motivation, and even physical health issues, making it even harder to stay productive.

Procrastination can be tricky—it's not always obvious why we put things off, but recognizing the patterns is the first step to breaking the cycle. Take a moment to really observe how you handle tasks. Do you find yourself delaying the same types of things over and over? Maybe it's responding to emails, starting a project, or even making decisions. If you're noticing these repeated habits, it could be a sign that something needs to shift.

The key is self-awareness; the more you understand your own procrastination patterns, the easier it is to tackle them head-on. Identifying the root cause makes it easier to create solutions that actually work. Whether it's setting small goals, creating a structured routine, or simply shifting your mindset, small changes can lead to big improvements.

Do you see yourself in these relevant snapshots of a procrastinator? Look, listen, and learn from these scenarios. The words and actions of a procrastinator:

The "I'll do it later" mantra: One of the most classic signs is the constant "I'll do it later" or "tomorrow" mantra. You'll hear someone say they really need to do something, but then you'll see them:

Getting super busy with less important stuff: This is often called "procrasti-working." They'll clean the entire house, organize their sock drawer, or respond to every non-urgent email, all to avoid the actual task. It looks like they're being productive, but they're just swapping one activity for another.

Finding endless distractions: Suddenly, social media, random YouTube videos, or even just staring out the window become incredibly compelling. It's like their brain is actively seeking anything to avoid the main event.

Making grand plans they don't follow through on: They might map out exactly how they're going to tackle the task, create elaborate to-do lists, or even set up their workspace perfectly. The intention is there, but the action is missing.

The "under pressure" justification: You might notice someone who consistently waits until the absolute last minute, then pulls an all-nighter to get things done. They might even claim they "work better under pressure." While a little adrenaline can be motivating, habitually relying on this usually leads to:

Rushed, lower-quality work: When you're scrambling, details can get missed, and the overall quality often suffers.

Increased stress and anxiety: This last-minute rush can be incredibly stressful, leading to burnout and a feeling of being constantly overwhelmed.

A cycle of guilt and self-reproach: After the task is done, there's often a feeling of "why did I put myself through that again?" which can feed into future procrastination.

"It's Too Much" Freeze: Sometimes, procrastination stems from feeling completely overwhelmed by a task. You might observe someone:

Becoming indecisive: They might struggle to even start because they don't know where to begin or how to break down a big project into smaller, manageable steps.

Expressing anxiety or fear: You might hear comments about how difficult the task is, how they might fail, or how they're worried about not doing it perfectly. This fear of not meeting expectations (their own or others') can be a huge paralyzer.

Avoiding the topic entirely: If you bring up the task, they might quickly change the subject or become visibly uncomfortable.

"Future Self Will Handle It" Delusion: This is a subtle one, but you'll notice it in the way people talk about future commitments. They might confidently agree to things, or tell themselves they'll easily manage a future workload, without fully accounting for current realities or the potential for their "future self" to feel just as unmotivated as their "present self." It's a common trick our brains play on us, making us believe that magically, tomorrow we'll have more energy or motivation.

"Always busy, never productive." This is when someone might be constantly doing something, but it's rarely the main task at hand. Think endless organizing of your workspace, deep diving into emails that aren't urgent, or suddenly needing to run errands.

Deadline adrenaline junkie: This happens when you delay until the very last minute, claiming they work best under pressure, but secretly it's just putting off the inevitable. It might show up as a lot of self-talk around perfectionism, where they convince themselves that they can't start until everything is absolutely perfect, which, of course, means never starting.

Then there's the **avoidance game** – lots of switching between tasks, checking social media every five minutes, or even physically removing themselves from the work environment. It's like their brain is trying every trick in the book to distract you from the real job. And finally, keep an eye out for a general sense of being overwhelmed or anxious about the task itself, which often leads to putting it off rather than facing it head-on.

We all do it sometimes, right? Putting things off, avoiding that one task that's looming over us. But when it becomes a regular thing, it's pretty interesting to be aware of personal patterns of procrastination. It's not about being lazy; there's often a lot more going on under the surface!

Observing these patterns can be really insightful, not just for others, but for ourselves too! Recognizing why we or someone else might be putting things off is often the first step to finding a way to get unstuck. It is possible to overcome procrastination.

By carefully observing these signs and asking yourself some important questions, you can gain a clearer understanding of whether procrastination is a problem in your life and begin to address its underlying causes. A checklist has been developed to help you assess your procrasti-pattern. Honestly deal with these questions and commit to overcoming procrastination based on your specific challenges. You can overcome procrastination.

To truly recognize your procrasti-patterns you must engage in some honest self-reflection.

Procrasti-Pattern Checklist

Do I frequently delay tasks despite knowing the negative consequences?
Do I often feel anxious or stressed about unfinished work?
Do I make excuses for why I haven't started or completed something?
Do I find myself doing other things when I know I should be working on a specific task?
Do I consistently wait until the last minute to tackle important responsibilities?
Do I often feel overwhelmed by the thought of starting a project?
Do I frequently underestimate the time it will take to complete tasks?
Do I believe I work better under pressure, even if the quality of my work suffers?
What emotions come up when I think about a task I'm avoiding (e.g., boredom, frustration, fear)?

Chapter 4: Identify the Root Cause

Okay, so why is it a big deal for you to personally figure out why you procrastinate? Imagine trying to fix a leaky faucet without knowing if it's a loose pipe, a worn-out washer, or a cracked fixture. You could try all sorts of random things, but you're probably just wasting time and effort. It's the same with procrastination! If you don't know the specific reason, you're putting things off; you're just throwing general "get productive" advice at a wall and hoping something sticks.

Maybe you're a perfectionist who's terrified of doing a bad job, so you never start. Or perhaps you're just overwhelmed by big tasks and don't know how to break them down. Maybe you find certain tasks incredibly boring and just can't bring yourself to do them. Once you pinpoint that personal root cause—whether it's fear, overwhelm, boredom, a need for novelty, or something else entirely—you can actually come up with targeted strategies that work for you. It's about getting to the heart of your specific struggle, so you can stop fighting against yourself and start making real progress!

Once you've recognized your problem, you can identify the root cause of your procrastination. For example, it might be fear of failure, lack of motivation, or feeling overwhelmed by everything you have to do. If it's fear, ask yourself why you're afraid. Why do you not want to do it? When you identify the underlying cause, it's time to develop a plan to overcome it.

To truly conquer procrastination, you need to play detective with your own habits and patterns. It's like unmasking the villain in your productivity story! Here's how you can start identifying those sneaky behaviors:

First, become an observer of your own actions. For a few days or a week, simply pay attention to when and why you procrastinate. When you find yourself putting something off, don't judge it, just notice it. What were you supposed to do? What did you do instead? What thoughts were going through your head at that moment? Were you feeling overwhelmed, bored, scared of not doing it perfectly, or just looking for a quick distraction? Keep a small log or a mental note of these instances.

Next, look for common threads. After a while, you'll start to see patterns emerge. Do you always put off tasks that seem "too big?" Do you tend to get sidetracked by social media when you're working on something complex? Do you avoid starting things if you're not sure how to do them perfectly? Is there a particular time of day when your procrastination monster rears its head?

Recognizing these recurring themes is the key to understanding your unique procrastination style.

Finally, dig a little deeper into the "why." Once you've identified the what and when, try to understand the why. For example, if you consistently put off big projects, is it because you're worried about failing? If you get distracted by your phone, is it because the task at hand feels boring or unpleasant?

Procrastination often serves as a way to avoid uncomfortable feelings. By pinpointing these underlying reasons, you gain valuable insight that empowers you to develop targeted strategies instead of just vaguely wishing you'd "do better." It's all about self-awareness, and once you know your enemy, you're halfway to defeating it!

Conquering procrastination is a personal victory and requires personal commitment. Figuring out why you procrastinate can take some time and deep thinking, but once you know the reason, you can begin making changes that will alter your life. Understanding why you procrastinate isn't always straightforward; it takes some real reflection and honesty with yourself. Maybe you hesitate because you worry your work won't be good enough, or you avoid a task because it feels too massive to tackle. Sometimes, putting things off is a way to dodge stress or discomfort, even when you know it's only making things worse in the long run.

The good news? Once you pinpoint the reason behind your procrastination, you can start making meaningful changes. Recognizing your patterns allows you to create better strategies, set realistic goals, and break tasks into smaller steps that feel more manageable. Over time, shifting your mindset and adjusting your habits can transform how you approach tasks—not just making you more productive, but also easing the stress that comes with procrastination. Figuring this out might take time, but it's worth it. Every small step toward change makes a difference. Use this checklist to keep you on track.

Why You Procrastinate and How It Affects You

Checklist

Are you a procrastinator? Please mark whichever applies.

- ☐ I find things to distract myself instead of doing the task.
- ☐ I put off starting or finishing tasks.
- ☐ I make excuses why I can't do a task.
- ☐ I wait until the last minute to finish a task.
- ☐ I miss deadlines.

Reasons

- ☐ I let emotions keep me from doing tasks.
- ☐ I tend to be resistant to doing tasks or projects.
- ☐ I let the environment dictate why or when I do a task.
- ☐ I let family obligations, circumstances or situations take precedence.
- ☐ I believe you inherited the procrastination gene, so you always procrastinate.
- ☐ I use fear or anxiety to procrastinate.
- ☐ I feel overwhelmed, so I procrastinate.
- ☐ I am overconfident or expect perfection, which keeps me from acting.
- ☐ I lack motivation and accountability. I'm indecisive or have abstract goals.
- ☐ I procrastinate because I don't like the task.
- ☐ I have ADHD or suffer from depression.
- ☐ I have low energy levels.

Harmful

- ☐ I experience stress-related problems.
- ☐ I experience a lack of self-control leading to other unhealthy habits.
- ☐ I experience a lack of a healthy social life, and friends/family avoid me.
- ☐ I underachieve and don't live up to my full potential.
- ☐ I don't have plans or goals, and I tend to drift through life.
- ☐ I lose jobs often or miss out on promotions.
- ☐ I'm frequently unhappy or unproductive.
- ☐ I am often self-critical and self-sabotaging.
- ☐ I feel shame, guilt, and disappointment in my life.

It's very easy to see how procrastination messes things up when you use a simple checklist! It helps to promote personal accountability and conscious awareness of how procrastination impacts your life.

Imagine you've got a task, big or small, that you're putting off. Instead of just letting it hang there, grab a piece of paper or open a note on your phone and list out a few things. First, jot down what negative consequences pop up because you're delaying. Maybe it's missing out on something fun later, feeling stressed and rushed, or even delivering something that's not your best work.

Then, think about the positive outcomes you're missing out on by not tackling it now. Could you have more free time, feel a sense of accomplishment, or even learn something new?

Now, compare those two columns. You will clearly notice that procrastination isn't just about putting things off: it's actively harming your peace of mind and potential!

Use the checklist and develop techniques to help you overcome procrastination. Overcoming procrastination starts with awareness and action. This checklist lets you recognize your procrastination patterns and take small, meaningful steps toward change. By identifying the tasks, you tend to delay, the emotions behind those delays, and the habits that reinforce procrastination, you can start building strategies to break the cycle.

Beyond the checklist, techniques like time blocking, breaking tasks into smaller steps, setting realistic deadlines, and minimizing distractions can help improve focus and efficiency. Using motivation boosters—like rewarding progress, changing your environment, or having an accountability partner—can also make a big difference.

The key is consistency. Small, intentional adjustments add up over time, helping you shift from procrastination mode to productivity.

You can do this!

Chapter 5: Find the Habit and Break the Cycle

It's not just about "trying harder" or "having more willpower." For sustained change, we absolutely must understand the specific habits and patterns that lead us to procrastinate. When you find the habit, you can break the cycle.

Procrastination is a coping mechanism used for adjusting to negative emotions. Understanding what triggers the habits that lead to procrastination will yield valuable insights into the problem. Procrastination patterns can expose deeper beliefs we hold about ourselves, the task, or success/failure. For example, consistently delaying writing might reveal a belief that "my writing isn't good enough."

Once you know why you procrastinate, you can implement specific, tailored strategies instead of generic advice. This process is fundamentally a self-knowledge exercise. The more you understand your own psychology, tendencies, and triggers, the more effectively you can manage your behavior.

Breaking Free from Procrastination Identifying and Overcoming Habits Worksheet

Realizing we have habits and patterns that makes us procrastinate is the first step in changing them. Use this worksheet to help you see what habits and patterns you need to put a stop to.

Recognition

What are you doing when you procrastinate? What situations cause you to procrastinate? And why are you procrastinating?

_____

_____

_____

_____

What excuses are you using? How can you break the excuses and begin the tasks?

_____

_____

_____

_____

Is it perfectionism or some other fear that stalls you? How can you get over wanting it to be perfect to help you move on?

_____

_____

_____

_____

Do you lack direction, use avoidance or become paralyzed by making a decision? How can you make this easier? What steps can you take to get moving?

_____

_____

_____

_____

Breaking Free

What steps can you take to get over what's holding you back? Are there people or resources that can help you?

_____

_____

_____

_____

Is your attitude part of the problem? How can you transform negative thoughts into positive actions? Are there affirmations you can say daily?

_____

_____

_____

_____

Does the problem stem from your role models you had growing up? What new role models can you emulate who are action takers?

_____

_____

_____

_____

What are some ways you can change your behavior? Can you write down all your tasks? Break them into smaller blocks of time?

_____

_____

_____

_____

What negative feelings do you have about tasks? How can you change or get rid of them?

_____

_____

_____

_____

How can you build your willpower against procrastination? How can you reduce your resistance to specific tasks?

_____

_____

_____

_____

Are you committed to breaking the cycle and to identifying ways to overcome procrastination?

_____

_____

_____

_____

Consider these suggestions to help you break the cycle of procrastination:

- **Break it Down:** Big tasks can feel scary. Try breaking big and complex projects into smaller, more manageable steps. Instead of "Write a report," think "Outline report," then "Write introduction," and so on. Each small win feels good and builds momentum!

- **Try the 2-Minute Rule:** If a task takes less than two minutes to do, do it immediately. Sending that email, washing that dish, or making that quick call – just get it done. It prevents small things from piling up.

- **Set a Deadline (and Stick to It!):** Give yourself a firm deadline, even if it's an artificial one. And tell someone about it! The accountability can be a powerful motivator.

- **Find Your Peak Productivity Time:** Are you a morning person or a night owl? Try to schedule your most demanding tasks during the time of day you feel most focused and energized.

- **Reward Yourself:** Once you complete a task you've been putting off, give yourself a little reward. It could be a short break, a favorite snack, or watching an episode of your favorite show. Positive reinforcement can be effective.

- **Eliminate Distractions:** Turn off notifications, close unnecessary tabs, and find a quiet space. Make it as easy as possible to focus.

- **Just Start (Seriously, Just Start!):** Sometimes the hardest part is actually starting the task. Tell yourself you'll work on it for just 15 minutes. Often, once you get going, you'll find it's not as bad as you thought, and you'll keep going.

- **Be Kind to Yourself:** Don't beat yourself up when you procrastinate. Acknowledge it, understand why it's happening, and then gently redirect yourself. Progress, not perfection, is the goal!

Remember, building new habits takes time and practice. Be patient with yourself, celebrate your small victories, and keep trying these strategies. You've got this!

Chapter 6: You Can Change Negative Habits

Break Tasks into Smaller Steps

Breaking tasks into smaller steps is very important when you're trying to kick procrastination to the curb! Think about it: a huge, daunting task can feel like climbing Mount Everest, and who wants to start that on a Tuesday morning? But if you break it down into tiny, manageable "hill climbs," suddenly it doesn't seem so overwhelming. Each little step you complete gives you a mini win, a little burst of dopamine that makes you feel good and motivates you to tackle the next bit. It's like building momentum, one tiny success after another, until you look back and realize you've conquered the whole mountain without even feeling like you were doing anything too hard. Plus, it makes it easier to figure out exactly where to start, which is often the biggest hurdle when you're dragging your feet.

Consider breaking the tasks into smaller, more manageable steps for everything you have to do. Breaking things down makes you feel less overwhelmed and makes it easier to get started.

Set Deadlines

We all know how easy it is to put things off, right? That's where setting deadlines comes in super handy. Think of them as friendly nudges that help us actually get things done instead of letting them hang over our heads forever. When you have a clear date staring you down, it creates a bit of healthy pressure that can kick your motivation into gear. It's not about being rigid, but more about giving yourself a clear finish line to aim for, which makes tackling those big tasks feel a lot less overwhelming. Plus, checking things off your list once a deadline is met feels amazing!

Setting deadlines is a potent motivator for overcoming procrastination. Setting specific deadlines for completing tasks allows you to hold yourself accountable and avoid putting things off. Try setting realistic deadlines and breaking tasks into smaller steps to make them more achievable.

For example, set a deadline to complete the research and gather all the necessary information in the first few days, then set another deadline for creating an outline by the end of the week. Now you can set a deadline for completing the first draft a few days later and a final deadline for editing and submitting the project. Take it one step at a time.

Use Positive Self-Talk

It's super important to sprinkle some positive self-talk into your routine, especially when you're battling the beast of procrastination! Think of it like being your own personal cheerleader instead of your harshest critic. When you're staring down a daunting task, it's easy for negative thoughts to creep in, like "I can't do this" or "I'll probably fail." Those thoughts just zap your motivation and make you want to put things off even more. But if you flip the script and tell yourself things like "I've got this!" or "Even a small step forward is progress," you start to build confidence and chip away at that mental wall.

Positive self-talk helps reframe the challenge, making it feel more manageable and less like an insurmountable mountain. It's all about shifting your mindset from dread to "let's do this!" and that little mental tweak can make all the difference in actually getting things done.

Negative self-talk is a significant barrier to doing what needs to be done and overcoming procrastination. Instead, try using positive self-talk to motivate yourself to remain focused on your goals. For example, instead of telling yourself, "I can't do this," try saying, "I can do this, and I will."

Minimize Distractions

Imagine you're trying to tackle that big project you've been putting off, right? Now, picture your phone buzzing every five minutes, your email chiming with new messages, and maybe your roommate asking you a question. It's like trying to navigate a maze while blindfolded!

Distractions are a primary source of procrastination. Minimizing those distractions is essential because every time your attention gets pulled away, even for a second, it takes mental effort to get back on track. It's like having to restart your brain and rebuild your focus from scratch, which just makes the task feel even more daunting and easier to avoid. By creating a distraction-free zone, you're essentially making it easier for your brain to stay focused and actually get things done, chipping away at that procrastination monster one focused chunk at a time. It's all about setting yourself up for success!

Try turning off your phone or closing your email while you work. Try working in a quiet space or using noise-canceling headphones to block distractions. Plus, set up these plans in advance so you can get to work immediately.

Reward Yourself

When it comes to tackling that pesky procrastination, one of the best tricks up your sleeve is actually rewarding yourself! Seriously, it sounds simple, but it's super effective. Think about it: if you've got something awesome waiting for you at the finish line, whether it's an episode of your favorite show, a yummy snack, or just some guilt-free scrolling time, suddenly that daunting task doesn't seem so bad. It transforms from this big, scary monster into a stepping stone to something you actually want to do. It's all about tricking your brain into associating productivity with pleasure, and before you know it, you're not just overcoming procrastination, you're practically looking forward to getting things done!

Rewarding yourself for completing tasks will motivate you to overcome your tendency for procrastination. Set small rewards for yourself for each milestone. Choose healthy breaks like walking after completing a task.

Get Support

So you know how sometimes you just can't seem to get started on something, even when you know you should? That's procrastination for you! But here's a little secret: getting some backup from your friends, family, or even a coach can be a total game-changer. Think of it like having a cheering squad or an accountability buddy. When you've got someone in your corner, they can help you break down big tasks into smaller, less scary steps. They can offer a fresh perspective, remind you of your "why," and even just listen to you vent when you're feeling overwhelmed. Plus, knowing someone is going to check in on your progress can be just the kick in the pants you need to actually do the thing. It's like having a built-in motivation machine that reminds you you're not alone in this struggle, and that alone can make all the difference!

Getting support from others is an invaluable tool for overcoming procrastination. For example, you might find a friend or family member who keeps you accountable or a coach or therapist who assists you with working through underlying issues.

Undoubtedly, overcoming procrastination is a challenge, but it's not impossible. With a bit of thoughtful action on your part, you will break the cycle of procrastination and start acting toward your goals.

The Procrastination Log/Tracker

Behavioral log trackers are fantastic tools for getting really specific about your procrastination habits. Here's how you can use one to pinpoint those patterns and behaviors:

1. The Procrastination Log/Tracker:

A Procrastination Log/Tracker can prove to be a helpful tool. A simple table with columns like:

o **Date/Time:** When did you intend to start the task? When did you actually start?

o **Task:** What was the specific task you were putting off? Be as detailed as possible (e.g., "Write first draft of history essay" instead of "Do homework")

o **Trigger:** What immediately preceded your procrastination? (e.g., "Opened email," "Felt overwhelmed," "Got a text message," "Stared at a blank screen").

o **Emotion/Feeling:** How were you feeling before you procrastinated? (e.g., "Anxious," "Bored," "Tired," "Uncertain," "Excited to do something else")

o **Procrastination Behavior:** What did you do instead of the task? (e.g., "Scrolled social media," "Watched YouTube," "Cleaned my room," "Ate a snack," "Talked to a friend")

- **Consequence (Immediate/Long-Term):** What happened because you procrastinated? (e.g., "Felt more stressed," "Had less time later," "Missed a deadline," "Task was rushed")
- **Alternative Action (What I could have done): What** could you have done differently to start or stay on track?

How to Use It:

For a week or two, every time you catch yourself procrastinating, fill out a row in this log. Don't judge yourself, just observe and record. The goal is to gather data, not to beat yourself up.

2. **Pattern Analysis Worksheet:**

After you've collected some data in your log, transfer the insights to a separate "Pattern Analysis" worksheet. This is where you look for themes. Create sections for:

- **Common Triggers:** Look at your "Trigger" column. Are there certain situations, times of day, or types of thoughts that consistently lead to procrastination? List them out (e.g., "Starting complex tasks," "After lunch slump," "Fear of failure").
- **Favorite Procrastination Activities:** What are your go-to distractions? (e.g., "Social media scrolling," "Netflix binging," "Excessive cleaning," "Checking emails unnecessarily")
- **Emotional Drivers:** What emotions frequently appear in your "Emotion/Feeling" column? Are you often

procrastinating when you feel anxious, bored, or perfectionistic?

- **Task Characteristics:** Are there specific types of tasks you always put off? (e.g., "Tasks without clear instructions," "Creative tasks," "Repetitive tasks," "Tasks I perceive as difficult")

How to Use It:

Go through your Procrastination Log and tally up or circle common entries in each of these categories. The more frequently something appears, the stronger the pattern.

3. **"Why I Procrastinate" Reflection Sheet:**

This worksheet encourages deeper introspection. For each identified pattern from your analysis, ask yourself:

- What is the underlying reason for this pattern? (e.g., "I avoid complex tasks because I'm afraid of making mistakes," "I scroll social media because I'm bored with the task," "I clean because it feels productive but avoids the real work")

- What belief might be fueling this? (e.g., "I believe I can only do good work under pressure," "I believe I'm not good enough to do this perfectly," "I believe this task is pointless") o   What am I gaining by procrastinating? (e.g., "Temporary relief from discomfort," "Avoiding potential failure," "A sense of control").

How to Use It:

Be brutally honest with yourself here. This is where you uncover the hidden benefits (often short-term and harmful long-term) that keep you stuck in the procrastination cycle.

By using a worksheet, you're not just vaguely thinking about procrastination; you're gathering concrete evidence, spotting recurring patterns, and digging into the "why" behind your behavior. This data-driven approach makes it much easier to come up with targeted, effective strategies to overcome your specific procrastination challenges!

Date/ Time	Task	Trigger	Emotion	Behavior	Consequence	Alternative Action

Overcoming Procrastination Habits and Patterns

"Not everything that is faced can be changed. But nothing can be changed until it is faced."

James Baldwin

We all occasionally put off doing something. When it becomes a habit and a pattern in our everyday existence, it becomes a problem.

I don't feel like... I don't want to... I'll do it tomorrow... These are all phrases that naturally come out of the procrastinator's mouth when they are faced with a task that needs to be done. They often come out sounding whiny with a "poor me" tone to them.

Procrastination happens to everyone, even those who are highly productive. The only difference is that a productive person can recognize their triggers that can lead them to procrastinate. Then, they learn how to beat procrastination using a calculated approach that includes why they procrastinate and then apply strategies to beat it.

Procrastination isn't just poor time management or laziness. It often comes from negative emotions that keep you hostage from taking action. People put things off because they're not in the right mood. Then they distract themselves with other tasks. By the time you realize what you are doing, you feel guilty for wasting so much time. Your mood worsens because you feel guilty. Your task deadline gets closer, and you feel worse.

This continual loop of self-destructive behavior can only be broken when you discover what is causing you to procrastinate.

Most of us experience guilt when we procrastinate. We become our own worst enemy. We know what we should be doing and what's in our best interest, but we don't follow through. The Greeks called it akrasia – the weakness of will; acting contrary to what we know is in our best interest.

Procrastinators are excellent at making excuses. The trick to beating procrastination is to recognize the habits and patterns that cause you to procrastinate and make changes that put a stop to the behavior.

We have learned why you procrastinate and how it can be harmful. Let's dig deeper into recognizing your procrastination habits and patterns and finding ways to put a halt to them.

Don't delay. Get started now.

Recognizing Procrastination Habits and Patterns

"I do my work at the same time each day—the last minute."

Source unknown

Because it is a fact that before you can beat procrastination, you have to recognize the habits and patterns of your own procrastination behavior, it is important to be reminded of your vulnerability factors.

You can do that by considering these three factors:

1. **When You Procrastinate** – Ask what situations cause you to procrastinate. Is it more at work or home? Do you struggle to finish tasks or to start them?

2. **How You Procrastinate** – Ask yourself what you do when you find yourself procrastinating. Are you stalking social media, watching TV or finding unimportant tasks to complete?

3. **Why You Procrastinate** – What is causing you to put off doing something? Are you distracted or do you feel overwhelmed?

Do you recognize yourself in any of these patterns?

- You fill your day with low-priority tasks or what you feel like doing at the moment.
- You leave important items on your To-Do list for a long time.
- You start a high-priority task but then go make coffee or surf social media.

- Find yourself reading emails several times without making a decision on what needs to be done.

- You think it has to be the right time to tackle a specific task.

- Notice you are doing unimportant tasks for other people instead of doing the important ones on your list.

- Tell yourself it's okay to put off doing something you're afraid to do. You think if you don't address it, it'll magically go away, or someone else will do it.

Each of these patterns leads to loss of productivity from procrastination. You probably have other habits or patterns that promote putting things off. Let's look at a few of them.

Making Excuses – People often come up with excuses or validations to justify their behavior. Each of these excuses, though, is simply that: an excuse. Are you using any of these excuses for not taking action?

- Not knowing how to do something, but afraid to or won't ask how.

- Not knowing what you need to do, not having a plan.

- Don't care when something gets done.

- Forgetting to do something, intentionally or not.

- Blaming sickness or bad health problems on the delay.

- Don't want to do something because it's boring, difficult, or not interesting.

- Don't care if it gets done or not.

- Using the habit of always waiting until the last minute to do something.

- Saying you work best under pressure.

- Had to do something else first before you could do the task.

- Blame it on lack of sleep, distractions, and family.

- I'll fail anyway, so why even start?

- I'm not a morning person. I'll do it later.

- This is more difficult for me than it is for others.

- Blaming our circumstances – I don't have an office, don't have all the things I need to do the task, and no one will leave me alone so I can work.

Perfectionism – Do you freeze up when it's time to start on a task or project because you know that it won't be perfect? If you think you can't do something until you can do it perfectly, it's a form of procrastination. And when we're waiting until the right moment to start- everything has to be perfect first, we may never start. How do you know it won't be good enough or perfect if you don't do it?

Avoidance Tactics – Are you putting off doing something because it's boring or unpleasant? This can be anything from paying bills to opening that letter from the government. Putting off tasks because we're not in the mood to do it is another form of avoidance.

Unorganized or Lack of Direction – Poor organization can lead to procrastination quickly. You might also be stuck because you don't know what steps to take to perform a task.

When you lack organizational skills or have a prioritized direction for your to-do list, you are more productive. You're more likely to feel less overwhelmed and find it easier to take action.

Analysis Paralysis – Do you find yourself overanalyzing how to do a task or make a decision? Overanalyzing something keeps you from taking any kind of action. Analysis paralysis can also come from having poor decision-making skills.

Uncomfortable Tasks – Fear of failing or succeeding keeps you from doing tasks that you don't know how to do. When you fear success, you're afraid you'll be swamped with requests to do even more tasks.

Useless Tasks – You spend a good part of each day checking Facebook, searching the internet for non-work-related stuff or working on easy tasks because they are simple to complete.

Delay Work and Decisions – Do you find yourself constantly putting off the work until the night before it's due? This pattern of procrastination keeps you stressed, in panic mode, and you may find yourself missing deadlines often.

We all have certain habits or ways of doing things that can hinder or help us in our daily productivity. Whether your procrastination habit or pattern is big or small, recognize it when you are doing it so you can begin taking steps to halt the behavior.

Halting Procrastination Habits and Patterns

"No more excuses or procrastination! Stop allowing your days to be stolen by busy nothingness and take calculated steps towards your goals."

Steve Maraboli

Once you clock the patterns and habits, you can begin putting a halt to them. You probably won't break them overnight, but you can begin by setting up strategies that will help you.

To get out of the routine and habit of habitually procrastinating, you have to create new routines and order in your life. Begin by taking small, daily steps in that direction.

Every day, simply tackle the task right in front of you. Then move on to the next one. It will require hard work and diligence, but the payoff is discipline, productivity, and happiness. You'll no longer be lost on what to do, and you will find life is much easier when you don't put things off or wait until the last minute.

If you have too many tasks to tackle or don't know what needs to be done, begin by listing all the tasks you need to do on a daily and weekly basis. Then write down the big tasks with their respective deadlines. Next, break big tasks into smaller ones.

Here are some tricks that might help on those deadline-oriented tasks:

- Set your deadline in your calendar for a few days before it's actually due. This tricks your mind into thinking it's due sooner.

- Commit to doing the tasks. Write the tasks down that you need to complete in your calendar with a specific time each day to do them. Give yourself a reward for completing a difficult job on time.

- Get an accountability partner to check up on you. Consider using an online tool like Procraster (http://procrasterapp.com/) to help self-monitor yourself.

- Tackle tasks as soon as they arise. Don't let them go for another day whenever possible.

- Turn your internal dialogue into positives. Instead of "need to" or "have to," say "I choose to," which implies that you are in control of your time.

- Get rid of distractions by turning off social media and email notifications.

- Do the most unpleasant tasks first thing each day or at your peak time.

- Focus on the long game, especially when doing unpleasant tasks. Identify the long-term benefits of completing the task. Also, identify the undesirable consequences of not doing the task as well.

- If procrastination is a problem because you are disorganized make it a point to implement strategies to get organized.

- Keep a to-do list so you don't conveniently forget tasks.

- Prioritize your to-do list for tasks you need to focus on first

- Learn to master scheduling and project planning so you can plan your time effectively. Use time-management and task-management apps to help you

- If overwhelm is causing you to delay projects, learn how to break them down into smaller, more manageable chunks. Focus on starting them, working in bursts. Or create an action plan to organize each step of the project.

- If analysis paralysis is keeping you from taking action, look at ways to help you make decisions and move on.

- You learned to procrastinate from your parents, siblings, or another person, who had an "I'll do it later" attitude. You need to think about the negative consequences they faced when they procrastinated. Find new role models to mimic, ones who are action takers and have positive results because of it.

- If you procrastinate because you don't think that you are good enough or you don't know how to do it, consider taking a course, asking for help or using self-affirming statements like "I can learn as I work on this."

- You procrastinated because you underestimated how quickly it would take you to do the task. You underestimate how long it takes as well as how quickly you can do it. Instead, start earlier than you think you need to and work on completing the project early.

- You think it has to be perfect, and it keeps you from getting started. Instead of emphasizing doing things perfectly, prioritize the importance of completing on time. Make a list of examples when your perfectionism was unhelpful and of the times when task completion was more helpful.

- You use your depression, anxiety or other condition as an excuse to delay tasks. If you know you have a condition that diminishes your motivation or concentration, get the proper treatment with a licensed therapist. They can help you set achievable goals for your condition and show you how to break your tasks into more manageable steps.

- You procrastinate because you compare yourself to others and find yourself lacking. Instead of comparing yourself, focus on improving yourself and doing your work to the best of your ability. That's all anyone asks of you.

- You procrastinate when you are not comfortable with the task or situation. Challenge yourself to step out of your comfort zone and engage in a task, even if it's only for a little while.

- You really just don't want to do the task that day. Instead of doing simpler or unrelated tasks, plan out the big task that needs doing and start it.

9 Ways to Change Your Behavior

"The really happy people are those who have broken the chains of procrastination, those who find satisfaction in doing the job at hand. They're full of eagerness, zest, and productivity. You can be, too."

Norman Vincent Peale

You recognize you have some habits and poor behavior patterns that are causing you to procrastinate on tasks. Here are 9 ways you can change your behavior to be more productive. You'll feel more confident, less stressed, and your reputation for completing tasks will improve.

1. Write down tasks that you've been putting off. This puts the project back in the front of your mind so you can't ignore it.

2. What are your feelings towards the task? Procrastination is an emotional reaction with three core emotions driving it. Do you fear that you won't get the task done on time or well enough? Are you angry because you are doing something you hate? Are you sad because you feel like you can't do the task? Dig down to identify the emotions behind your procrastination pattern.

3. Now get rid of those emotions. Do what you need to so you can release the emotions before they build up inside you. In private, shiver to get rid of fear, stomp around to release anger or have a good cry to release sadness.

4. Turn destructive thinking into something constructive. If the task you need to do brings about negative thoughts, find an alternative positive way of seeing the task.

5. Break big tasks down into a series of small, doable steps. Map out each part of the project.

6. Congratulate yourself on each small step you accomplish. Reward yourself in some way. This motivates you and helps keep fear at bay.

7. Anticipate obstacles that could pop up along the way to completing the task.

8. Take action on the steps or task you've been putting off. Fight any resistance you have about doing it. Fight excuses, bad moods or other discouragements you might want to use to keep from doing the task.

9. Finish the daunting task and enjoy the win. Accomplishing what you were once avoiding can simplify your work or personal life, giving you more energy, better sleep and a feeling of success.

When it comes to changing your behavior from procrastinating to productive accomplishment, it means taking responsibility for your thoughts and actions while forcing yourself to follow through with the guidelines you create for yourself.

When it comes to changing your behavior from one of procrastinator to productive accomplishment, it means taking responsibility for your thoughts and actions while forcing yourself to follow through.

Encouragement for Procrastinators

"Don't wait. The time will never be just right."

Napoleon Hill

Procrastinators are big avoiders. They use excuses to keep validating why they don't begin or finish tasks. They find it difficult to make decisions. It can stem from many things, as we've seen, such as laziness, perfectionism, fear, or depression.

- First, forgive yourself for procrastinating. This helps you feel more positive about yourself. It may also help you reduce the chances of procrastinating in the future.

- It's okay to struggle, but be intentional about finding something that works for you.

- Remember, you are not the only person who procrastinates, fears, struggles, finds things difficult to do, or feels bored with certain tasks. Reach out to others for encouragement.

- Practice doing what feels difficult or out of your comfort zone every day. It helps you overcome the difficulty and build confidence in your abilities.

- For each task you complete, you're building good habits and setting good examples for others.

- You'll feel less frazzled and more at peace when you change your habits to being productive over avoidance.

- It doesn't have to be perfect.

- By doing what you are supposed to do when you're supposed to do it, you gain the freedom to relax or do what you enjoy.

- You are worth it. The work you do is worth it.

- You can do it.

- Use affirmations to keep your thoughts positive about tasks you don't enjoy.

Next Steps

Make no mistake about it. Bad habits are called 'bad' for a reason. They kill our productivity and creativity. They slow us down. They hold us back from achieving our goals. And they're detrimental to our health.

John Rampton

Successful people don't make excuses. They simply push past it. The best way to stop procrastinating is to keep it out of your life. But if you're already a chronic procrastinator, you can get rid of procrastination by making small, meaningful changes.

Begin by writing out tomorrow's schedule and to-do list. Create a schedule for every task on your list and hold yourself accountable in some way. Imagine how great you will feel once you have accomplished the tasks.

Overcoming procrastination habits and patterns takes willpower and finding ways to reduce the resistance you have to the task.

You can build your willpower by:

- Meditation and prayer
- Using mindfulness techniques
- Having self-compassion and forgiving yourself
- Managing your energy levels
- Time management techniques
- Exercising
- Reducing your decision-making fatigue

You can reduce your resistance by:

- Setting timers
- Focusing on just getting started
- Lowering your standards
- Breaking complex tasks into smaller steps
- Using blocks of time to complete tasks
- Setting up a schedule to complete projects
- Having an accountability partner or app

Breaking your procrastination habits and patterns requires that you actively think about why and when you procrastinate. When you catch yourself making an excuse, for example, you are starting to break the habit of procrastination.

Now that you know what you need to do to halt your procrastination in its tracks, don't wait. Start with one task right now that you can finish quickly. Now let's go to the next session to learn about becoming more productive to beat procrastination.

Stop Letting Procrastination Stall Your Success

Procrastination is a common enemy. Ask ten people, and more than likely, they will list procrastination as to why they didn't get to something earlier or why they haven't accomplished their goals yet. Procrastination can easily stall success because:

- It leads to missed opportunities.
- It ruins your reputation and trustworthiness.
- It stunts productivity and creativity.
- It creates complacency and stressful environments.

Procrastination is self-sabotage. There is no value to it, no matter how much you tell yourself there is. You may think it provides the motivation and inspiration you need to get moving, but you are only hindering your creativity and ability to perform well.

When you procrastinate, you are sabotaging yourself, and you rush, which causes you to make mistakes and avoid essential details, ultimately affecting the quality of your work. Don't feel guilty or discouraged if you suffer from procrastination. You are not alone, and fortunately, you can do something about it with a little hard work and dedication.

Recognize Your Fears or Resistance

Procrastinating is not the reason you are delaying your work. It's the reaction or actions you are taking due to your resistance. It could be the fear of failure, the fear of success, or the judgment holding you back. It could also be because you are going after the wrong goals that don't make you happy or feel successful.

There are so many "ifs" that could be listed, but the vital thing to note is that only you really know what it is. Please take a moment to recognize those feelings and intrusive thoughts as they are happening to identify them truly. Avoiding your resistance or fears will only feed your procrastination.

Don't Wait for It to Feel Right

Sometimes in life, you must do things that are uncomfortable or when you don't feel like it.

The main difference between a successful business and an unsuccessful business is persistence, the ability to keep pushing forward no matter the obstacles that lie ahead.

Remember and Imagine Your Future

Overcoming Procrastination

Comfort now doesn't mean you will be comfortable in the future. Procrastination is about avoiding or delaying discomfort. Yet comfort won't and can't always be consistent, as persistence and consistency are needed to be successful long term. The more you imagine your future, the better you can manage your time now. When you realize and remember that the actions you take now directly influence your comfort in the future, you will make better decisions. Remember, procrastination is as much a symptom as it is a culprit hindering your success. To overcome it, you must look beyond it, make the commitment to change, and always take action. Persistence and consistency are keys to success, don't give in to procrastination, or you will risk stalling your success and sabotaging your destiny.

Becoming More Productive and Overcoming Procrastination Checklist

Being more productive keeps you from procrastinating. Use this checklist to keep you on track to avoid procrastination. Add your own sentences to the empty spaces to customize this list.

Becoming More Productive

- ☐ I made a reasonable to-do list with 3 to 5 similar tasks.
- ☐ I set small goals or steps for larger projects.
- ☐ I focus on one big goal at a time.
- ☐ I break big tasks into smaller ones.
- ☐ I track my time.
- ☐ I delegate work to others.
- ☐ I know what my peak hours are.
- ☐ I work on one task at a time.
- ☐ I decluttered and cleared away distractions.
- ☐ I fit in exercise every day.
- ☐ I work on similar tasks together, such as answering all emails.
- ☐ _____
- ☐ _____
- ☐ _____
- ☐ _____

Improve Productivity

- ☐ I break big projects into smaller tasks.
- ☐ I use the 7-minute rule to get started.
- ☐ I used cues to help me build better habits.
- ☐ I use rewards when I finish a big project.
- ☐ I ask for help when I need it.
- ☐ I work on tasks that match my mood.
- ☐ _____
- ☐ _____
- ☐ _____
- ☐ _____

Strategies

- ☐ I set reasonable daily goals.
- ☐ I schedule tasks into a daily, weekly, and monthly calendar/planner.
- ☐ I chunk work into bite-sized tasks.
- ☐ I take short breaks to refresh my mind and body.
- ☐ I prioritize my tasks.
- ☐ _____
- ☐ _____
- ☐ _____
- ☐ _____

Tools

- ☐ I use a scheduler.
- ☐ I use project management tools.
- ☐ I implement time management software.
- ☐ I use calendars.
- ☐ I use journals and planners.
- ☐ I use tools for organizing and keeping notes.
- ☐ _____
- ☐ _____
- ☐ _____
- ☐ _____

Becoming More Productive and Overcoming Procrastination Worksheet

Being more productive and successful is the best way to avoid procrastination. Use this worksheet to help you identify and develop specific ways for you to be more productive.

Consider: What do you need to begin a task or project? Do you have the task scheduled and added to your to-do list? Is your to-do list small enough that you can reasonably accomplish what's on it each day? Did you include 3 to 5 top-priority tasks?

_____

_____

_____

_____

_____

_____

_____

_____

Consider: What goals have you set for your projects, tasks, or goals? What steps do you need to take for each one?

_____

_____

_____

_____

_____

Consider: Are you trying to complete more than one big goal or project at a time? What can you do to put all of them off while you work on the highest priority one? Give some to someone else, ask for help, or hire help?

_____

_____

_____

_____

_____

Consider: Are you tracking how much time you're spending or wasting on certain tasks? Which ones? Are you working on high-priority or harder tasks during your peak hours? What are your peak working hours? Note details.

_____

_____

_____

_____

_____

Consider: What can you do to clear the clutter and chaos in your work area, your home and anywhere that is causing you to procrastinate? Is exercise, healthy eating and taking time to rejuvenate a part of your day?

_____

_____

_____

_____

_____

Consider: How can you improve your productivity? Break projects into smaller tasks? Do something for seven minutes just to get started? Give yourself clues and rewards to help you begin a new habit or finish a task? Work when your mood is in sync?

_____

_____

_____

_____

_____

Consider: What strategies will you implement to enable you to become more productive?

_____

_____

_____

_____

_____

Consider: Are there any resources you can put into place to make productivity easier? What apps, tools or software can you use? Do you need time or project management software? Which ones? Which fits your needs: digital or paper; planners or calendars?

_____

_____

_____

_____

_____

Is Validation Holding You Back from Success?

The need for validation and procrastination are often intertwined, both stemming from underlying fears, self-doubt, or a desire for perfection. Addressing both requires a multi-faceted approach focusing on self-compassion, self-efficacy, and practical strategies.

Addressing the Need for Validation:

The constant need for external validation can be exhausting and limit your authentic self-expression. Here are ways to address it:

Examine the Root Cause:

Childhood Experiences: Reflect on your early life experiences. Did you receive conditional love or approval? Understanding these patterns can shed light on your current need for external validation.

Childhood experiences can profoundly shape an individual's psychological landscape, leading to a deep-seated need for validation and contributing to patterns of procrastination in adulthood. This connection often stems from early emotional environments that impact self-worth, fear of failure, and the ability to self-regulate.

Here's how these factors intertwine:

Childhood Experiences and the Need for Validation

A strong need for external validation often originates from childhood experiences where a child's sense of worth was contingent on external factors, such as:

Overly Critical or Demanding Parents: Children raised by parents who were consistently critical, set unrealistic expectations, or rarely offered praise might internalize the belief that they are "never good enough." They learn that their value comes from achieving perfection or avoiding mistakes, leading to a constant search for approval from others.

Lack of Attention or Emotional Neglect: When children don't receive sufficient emotional attention, affirmation, or validation of their feelings, they may grow up feeling invisible or unimportant. As adults, they might seek this missing validation from others, believing that if they can just get others' approval, they will finally feel seen and valued.

Conditional Love/Praise for Perfection: If love, attention, or praise were only given when a child achieved specific outcomes (e.g., perfect grades, winning competitions), they learn to associate their worth with their accomplishments. This can instill a belief that they must always be perfect to be loved or accepted, making external validation a primary driver.

Unstable or Unpredictable Environments: Growing up in chaotic or unpredictable homes can lead to a sense of insecurity. Children in such environments might try to "people-please" or gain approval as a survival mechanism, hoping to maintain peace or secure a sense of safety. This can manifest as an ingrained habit of bending over backwards for others in adulthood.

Suppressed Emotions: If children were discouraged from expressing their true emotions ("boys don't cry," "don't be angry"), they might learn to invalidate their own feelings. As adults, they may then seek external validation for their emotions, needing others to confirm that their feelings are legitimate.

Insecure Attachment Styles: Children who experience inconsistent or unreliable caregiving may develop insecure attachment styles (anxious, avoidant, or disorganized). This can lead to low self-esteem and a strong reliance on external approval to regulate their sense of self.

How the Need for Validation Contributes to Procrastination

The deeply ingrained need for validation can significantly fuel procrastination through several mechanisms:

Fear of Failure and Perfectionism:

If one's self-worth is tied to external approval, the fear of not meeting expectations (and thus losing that approval) becomes immense. This can lead to perfectionism, where the pressure to perform flawlessly is so paralyzing that tasks are avoided altogether. Procrastination becomes a way to delay the moment of potential judgment or failure.

Fear of Judgment and Criticism:

Similar to the fear of failure, the fear of being judged or criticized by others can cause individuals to put off tasks. If they anticipate negative feedback, they might delay starting or completing a project to postpone the discomfort of potential disapproval.

Self-Handicapping:

Procrastination can be a form of "self-handicapping." By delaying a task until the last minute, individuals create an external excuse for poor performance. If they fail, they can attribute it to a lack of time rather than a lack of ability, thus protecting their fragile self-esteem and the potential for negative validation.

Analysis Paralysis:

The desire for a perfect outcome to secure validation can lead to overthinking, overplanning, and an inability to start. The individual gets stuck in the planning phase, constantly seeking more information or trying to anticipate every possible problem, rather than taking action.

Prioritizing Others' Needs:

Individuals with a strong need for validation, especially those with people-pleasing tendencies, might prioritize tasks that will gain them approval from others over their own important work. This can lead to neglecting personal responsibilities and procrastinating on tasks that don't have immediate external rewards.

Anxiety and Overwhelm:

The pressure to be perfect and gain validation can lead to high levels of anxiety around tasks. This anxiety can be overwhelming, making it difficult to initiate or focus on work, leading to avoidance and procrastination.

In essence, childhood experiences can create a fragile sense of self-worth that is heavily reliant on external affirmation. When faced with tasks that carry the risk of judgment or failure, this ingrained need for validation can trigger protective mechanisms like procrastination, offering a temporary escape from potential disapproval but ultimately hindering progress and personal growth.

Fear of Abandonment/Rejection:

Often, seeking validation is a way to ensure you're liked and accepted, preventing potential abandonment or rejection. Acknowledge this fear.

Low Self-Worth:

If you don't believe in your own worth, you'll constantly look to others to confirm it.

Prevents You from Being Your True and Honest Self

When you are always worried about impressing others, you are also pushing your true self away. This also means that no matter who you talk to, you will be someone different. You will simply reflect the person you are talking to and not yourself.

It Breeds Perfectionism and Procrastination

You cannot be perfect. No one is. And no, they're not perfect, even if they look shiny and perfect. Work toward being your best self, but accept that your best self includes making mistakes. There is a high probability that you also experience procrastination, which can negatively affect your personal and professional life.

With procrastination, there is always compromise. Procrastination often stems from fear of failure, meaning you put off the work as not doing it at all is better than disappointment.

However, only through disappointment and stepping outside of your comfort zone do you positively grow as a person.

You Can't and Won't Make Everyone Happy

It's natural to want validation, but impossible to receive or expect it from everyone. If you let this happen, you will never be successful, as you constantly have your mindset on the wrong goals and aspirations. You are responsible for your happiness. Make sure you are doing exactly what needs to be done to get there, and don't let distractions like this get in your way.

Cultivate Self-Validation

Practice Self-Care:

Engage in activities that nourish you mentally, emotionally, and physically. This reinforces your inherent worth.

Positive Affirmations:

Regularly tell yourself you are proud, capable, and worthy. Tailor these to your specific needs.

Accept Your Feelings Without Judgment:

Understand that all feelings, even negative ones, are normal. Don't seek external reassurance that your feelings are "okay."

Focus on Progress, Not Perfection:

Celebrate your small achievements and acknowledge how far you've come.

Treat Yourself Like a Friend:

If a friend were struggling, how would you speak to them? Apply that same kindness and understanding to yourself.

Develop an Inner Compass:

Listen to your intuition and trust your own judgment. What feels right to you?

Manage External Interactions

Practice Saying No:

Start with small requests and gradually work your way up. This sets boundaries and reinforces your autonomy.

Surround Yourself with Nourishing Support:

Seek out people who genuinely support and uplift you, rather than those who might exploit your vulnerability.

Detach from Invalidating People:

If certain individuals consistently make you feel small or invalidate your experiences, limit your interactions with them.

Reduce Comparisons:

Social media often fuels the need for validation by encouraging constant comparison. Limit your exposure to content that makes you feel inadequate.

Seek Professional Help:

If the need for validation is deeply ingrained and significantly impacting your life, a therapist can help you explore its origins and develop healthier coping mechanisms.

Breaking Free from Procrastination

Procrastination often stems from fear (of failure, success, judgment), perfectionism, or a lack of motivation. Here are strategies to overcome it:

Understand Your Procrastination Style

Identify the "Why:"

Are you procrastinating due to fear of failure, fear of success, perfectionism, low self-efficacy, task aversiveness, or impulsivity? Understanding the underlying reason is crucial.

Awareness:

Pay attention to your habits and thoughts that lead to procrastination. What feelings do you experience before you procrastinate?

Make Tasks More Manageable and Appealing

Break Down Tasks:

Large, overwhelming tasks become less intimidating when broken into smaller, actionable steps.

Set Clear, Achievable Goals:

Vague goals are easy to put off. Define what success looks like for each task.

The 2-Minute Rule:

If a task takes two minutes or less, do it immediately. This builds momentum.

Gamify Your Behavior:

Incorporate elements from games, like points or streaks, to make tasks more engaging.

Reward Accomplishments:

Give yourself small, immediate rewards for completing tasks or milestones. This creates positive reinforcement.

Make it Less Aversive:

Find ways to make unpleasant tasks more tolerable. Can you listen to music while doing it? Can you change your environment?

Boost Self-Efficacy and Confidence

Focus on the "Next Action:"

Instead of dwelling on the entire project, identify the very next physical action you need to take.

Build Momentum:

Starting with easy tasks can create a sense of accomplishment and make it easier to tackle harder ones.

Visualize Success:

Imagine yourself successfully completing the task and the positive feelings that come with it.

Focus on What You Want to Do:

Shift your mindset from avoiding a task to achieving a positive outcome.

Implement Time Management and Accountability

Set Deadlines (Self-Imposed):

Treat your self-imposed deadlines as seriously as external ones.

Prioritize Tasks:

Use tools like the Eisenhower Matrix (urgent/important) to focus on high-priority items.

Time Management Techniques:

Experiment with methods like the Pomodoro Technique (focused work intervals with breaks).

Minimize Distractions:

Create a dedicated workspace, turn off notifications, and use website blockers if necessary.

Develop Accountability:

Share your goals and progress with a trusted friend, mentor, or accountability partner.

Practice Self-Compassion

Forgive Yourself:

Don't beat yourself up for past procrastination. Self-criticism often leads to more procrastination. Forgive yourself and focus on moving forward.

Be Kind to Yourself:

Recognize that procrastination is a common human struggle. Treat yourself with understanding, especially when facing setbacks.

Challenge Self-Critical Thoughts

Replace negative self-talk with kinder, more positive ways to motivate yourself.

By working on both your need for validation and your procrastination habits, you can build a stronger sense of self-worth and become more productive and fulfilled.

Validation is the process of making sure you are right or valued in some way. It's often what people think they need to feel accepted by the world. In small doses, it's healthy and makes sense to want to feel this way; however, it's often the key holding people back from success.

Seeking validation can definitely be a sneaky saboteur when it comes to chasing your dreams. Think about it: if you're constantly waiting for someone else to give you the green light, tell you you're good enough, or approve of your ideas, you're essentially putting your progress on hold. This can easily spiral into procrastination because you might feel paralyzed until you get that external stamp of approval. It's like you're stuck at the starting line, even if you're perfectly capable of running the race on your own. Breaking free from this cycle means trusting your own judgment and taking action, even if no one's cheering you on just yet!

Envy and Comparison Lead to Failure

You are different from everyone else, and that is a beautiful thing. Only you can be who you are, in the same way, you are you. That alone should make you feel proud. Understanding that no one is better than the other is essential because you don't want to compare yourself unrealistically.

Envy and comparison are potent psychological forces that can subtly, and sometimes not so subtly, steer individuals towards failure and procrastination. Let's break down how these two interconnected elements contribute to such negative outcomes.

How Envy and Comparison Lead to Failure:

Distorted Goals and Priorities: When we constantly compare ourselves to others, especially those we perceive as more successful, we risk adopting their goals instead of defining our own. This leads to pursuing paths that don't align with our true passions, strengths, or values. Working towards something we don't genuinely desire is a recipe for disengagement, mediocrity, and ultimately, failure to achieve meaningful personal success.

Unrealistic Expectations and Disappointment: Social media, in particular, often presents a curated highlight reel of others' lives. Comparing our struggles and everyday realities to these idealized versions inevitably leads to unrealistic expectations for our own progress.

When we don't achieve results as quickly or seamlessly as we imagine others have, we become easily discouraged, leading to feelings of inadequacy and a greater likelihood of giving up.

Wasted Energy and Diminished Focus: The act of envying and comparing consumes valuable mental and emotional energy that could otherwise be directed towards productive work. Instead of focusing on our own tasks, improving our skills, or strategizing for the future, we're preoccupied with what others have, how they got it, and how we measure up. This fragmented focus hinders progress and makes it difficult to commit fully to our own endeavors.

Paralysis by Analysis and Self-Doubt: Constant comparison can lead to an overwhelming sense of not being good enough. This self-doubt can be paralyzing, making us hesitant to take risks, try new things, or even start a project because we fear we won't measure up to some perceived standard set by others. This "analysis paralysis" prevents action and, consequently, prevents success.

Competitive Sabotage (of Self): While healthy competition can be motivating, envy-driven comparison often morphs into a destructive internal competition. Instead of focusing on self-improvement, the goal becomes "beating" or "keeping up with" others. This can lead to unhealthy shortcuts, unethical behavior, or simply diverting energy away from genuine growth towards superficial achievements, ultimately undermining long-term success.

How Envy and Comparison Lead to Procrastination:

Overwhelm and Intimidation:

Seeing others seemingly effortlessly achieve great things can make our own tasks seem daunting and insurmountable. If someone else's output appears better, the thought of starting our own "inferior" work can be paralyzing, leading us to avoid it altogether. The fear of not being able to measure up can be a powerful driver of procrastination.

Perfectionism as a Defense Mechanism:

Comparison often fuels perfectionism. If we believe everyone else is doing things flawlessly, we might feel immense pressure to do the same. This can lead to endless tweaking, re-doing, and a refusal to release anything until it's "perfect," which often means it's never released at all. Procrastination becomes a way to delay the inevitable moment of perceived imperfection.

Loss of Intrinsic Motivation:

When our motivation shifts from internal satisfaction and personal growth to external validation and keeping up with others, our intrinsic drive diminishes. Work that was once enjoyable becomes a chore, driven by obligation or fear of inadequacy. This lack of genuine enthusiasm makes it easier to put off tasks.

Fear of Failure (in Comparison):

The fear of not measuring up to others' standards can be so strong that it's easier to simply not start. If we don't attempt something, we can't fail (at least not in the eyes of others or our own self-critical internal voice). Procrastination becomes a protective shield against the potential embarrassment or disappointment of not comparing favorably.

Diminished Self-Efficacy:

Repeatedly comparing ourselves unfavorably to others erodes our belief in our own abilities. When we don't believe we can succeed, the motivation to even begin a task wanes significantly. Why bother starting if we're convinced we'll fail anyway? This self-fulfilling prophecy of low self-efficacy is a prime driver of procrastination.

Breaking the Cycle:

To counteract these negative effects, it's crucial to cultivate:

Self-Awareness: Recognize when you're engaging in unhelpful comparison.

Gratitude: Focus on what you have and what you've achieved.

Define Your Own Success: Set goals based on your values and passions, not others' perceived achievements.

Celebrate Small Wins: Acknowledge your own progress, no matter how incremental.

Focus on Growth, Not Perfection: Embrace the process of learning and improvement.

Limit Exposure to Triggers: Be mindful of social media and other sources that fuel comparison.

Practice Self-Compassion: Be kind to yourself, recognizing that everyone's journey is unique.

In essence, envy and comparison are distractions that pull us away from our own path. By focusing inward, on our unique strengths, goals, and progress, we can break free from their detrimental grip and move towards genuine achievement and fulfillment.

It is also important to note that blending in and ensuring you don't look abnormal doesn't always equal validation. It's okay to value the opinions or perspectives of others, but do not allow them to control you. Due to this fact, it's even more important to live each day honestly and value yourself. When you do find that validation, you know in your soul that it's genuine and honest.

Impacts Quality of Work

Validation is a vulnerability that can put you on the wrong path. It could distract you from what is essential, which is accomplishing your goal. Validation can lead to a lesser quality of work and lackluster results. How can you expect yourself to do "A" plus when you are not being authentic with yourself?

Be authentic. Be you. Learn to validate yourself and encourage yourself. Evaluate your actions, ensuring they match your stated values, to ensure you don't let validation hold you back from success.

If you always go back to think about what other people are thinking or stop what you are doing due to fear of judgment, then you will lose your momentum. As hard as it may be to believe, you don't need validation to be successful.

Overcoming Procrastination through Scriptural Mindfulness, Prayer and Meditation

Have you heard of the practice of scriptural mindfulness, prayer and meditation? By practicing scriptural mindfulness, prayer and meditation, you can reduce stress, improve your focus and motivation, and gain a greater sense of control over your thoughts and emotions. In this discussion, we'll explore how scriptural mindfulness, prayer, and meditation can help you overcome procrastination and provide some tips and ideas for incorporating these practices into your daily routine.

What is Scriptural Mindfulness, Prayer and Meditation?

Scriptural Mindfulness is all about being present in the moment and adjusting your thoughts and feelings on the foundation of that truth. It's about aligning your thoughts and feelings to affirm your commitment to inner peace. Scriptural mindfulness helps you gain insight into your emotions and develop greater awareness of your thoughts and actions. It is your personal agreement with biblical principles.

Meditation is a form of mindfulness that involves focusing your attention on a specific lesson, thought, or activity to improve your mental clarity and relaxation. It helps you reduce stress, improve your focus, and gain greater control over your thoughts and emotions.

How Scriptural Mindfulness and Meditation Can Help You Overcome Procrastination?

There are several benefits of using mindfulness and meditation in your daily life to overcome procrastination. Read these scenarios and consider how using this technique could help you.

1. Scriptural mindfulness and meditation can help reduce stress and anxiety, which can be major contributors to procrastination. For example, consider the story of Sarah, a busy mom who was feeling overwhelmed with work and family responsibilities. She started practicing scriptural mindfulness and meditation. Soon, she noticed a significant reduction in her stress and anxiety levels. As a result, she was better able to focus on her tasks and make progress towards her goals.

2. Scriptural mindfulness and meditation can help you improve your focus and motivation, which are critical for overcoming procrastination. Jason, a student who was struggling to stay focused on his studies, started practicing scriptural mindfulness and meditation regularly. He soon noticed a significant improvement in his focus and motivation. He was able to complete his assignments more quickly and with greater ease, and ultimately achieved better grades.

Scriptural mindfulness and meditation can help you gain greater self-awareness and insight into your thoughts and emotions. For example, a friend of mine, Emily, struggled with procrastination and felt like she was always putting things off. She started practicing scriptural mindfulness and meditation every day. She was able to gain a greater insight into her thought patterns and emotions. This helped her to understand why she was procrastinating and develop strategies to overcome it.

Tips for Integrating Scriptural Mindfulness and Meditation into Your Routine

Now that you know what scriptural mindfulness and meditation are and how they can help overcome stress, you need to know how to integrate them into your routine.

Start Small.

Start with just a few minutes of scriptural mindfulness or meditation each day, and gradually increase the time as you become more comfortable.

Find a Quiet Location.

Find a quiet place where you can focus and avoid distractions. This could be a park, a quiet room in your home, or simply a quiet corner of your office.

Use Scripture to Guide Your Meditations.

If you're new to scriptural meditation, consider using a modern translation of scripture to guide your meditation to help you get started. There are many apps and online resources available that offer a modern translation to easily understand the scriptures for guided meditations.

Make it a Habit.

Make scriptural mindfulness and meditation a habit by incorporating them into your daily routine. For example, you might meditate for 10 minutes each morning before starting your day, or practice mindfulness while taking a walk in the park.

Scriptural mindfulness and meditation are powerful tools that can help you overcome procrastination and achieve your goals. By reducing stress, improving focus and motivation, and increasing self-awareness, these practices can help you be more productive and focused. So, give it a try and see the difference they can make in your life.

Renewing the Mind: Scriptures often speak to the importance of transforming one's mind. For instance, Romans 12:2 (NIV) states,

"Do not conform to the pattern of this world, but be transformed by the renewing of your mind." When applied to procrastination, this means consciously replacing patterns of avoidance and delay with thoughts rooted in diligence, responsibility, and purpose, as encouraged by scripture.

Identifying Root Causes: Many scriptures address themes related to laziness, idleness, and lack of discipline, but also diligence, faithfulness, and stewardship. By mindfully examining these passages, individuals can gain insight into the spiritual and psychological roots of their procrastination. Is it fear of failure? A lack of self-worth? A misunderstanding of their divine purpose?

Finding Motivation and Encouragement: Scriptural texts are replete with stories and verses that inspire perseverance, hard work, and the rewards of diligence. Philippians 4:13 (NIV), "I can do all this through him who gives me strength," is a powerful example that can be brought to mind when feeling overwhelmed by a task.

Cultivating a Sense of Responsibility: Many scriptures emphasize accountability and the importance of using one's time and talents wisely. Understanding that one's abilities are a gift can foster a sense of responsibility that combats the tendency to squander time.

Prayer: Invoking Divine Assistance and Guidance

Prayer is a direct communication with the divine, a means of seeking strength, wisdom, and intervention. When facing procrastination, prayer can be a powerful tool for shifting one's mindset and gaining the resolve needed to act.

Seeking Strength and Discipline: Procrastination often stems from a perceived lack of strength or discipline. Through prayer, individuals can specifically ask for these qualities. A prayer might be, "God, grant me the discipline to start this task and the focus to complete it."

Overcoming Fear and Anxiety: Fear of failure, judgment, or the sheer magnitude of a task can be major drivers of procrastination. Prayer offers an avenue to release yourself from the stress and trust in divine support and reassurance. "Lord, release me from the fear that holds me back, and grant me peace to move forward."

Gaining Clarity and Wisdom: Sometimes, procrastination arises from not knowing where to start or feeling overwhelmed by complexity. Prayer can be a way to ask for clarity and divine wisdom in approaching a task, breaking it down, or finding the right resources.

Expressing Intent and Commitment: Articulating one's intentions and commitment to overcome procrastination through prayer can solidify those desires and create a deeper sense of accountability, not just to oneself, but to the creator.

Meditation: Cultivating Inner Stillness and Focus

Meditation, in this context, involves quiet contemplation, focusing the mind, and often incorporating scriptural truths. It's about training the mind to be present and to direct attention intentionally.

Mindful Breathing and Presence: Simple breathing exercises can ground an individual in the present moment, pulling them away from the distracting thoughts of past failures or future anxieties that often fuel procrastination. By focusing on the breath, one can learn to observe urges to procrastinate without immediately acting on them.

Scriptural Visualization and Affirmation: During meditation, one can visualize oneself diligently working on tasks, successfully completing them, and experiencing the positive outcomes. This can be coupled with repeating scriptural affirmations that reinforce diligence, focus, and divine strength (e.g., "I am capable through God who strengthens me").

Developing Self-Awareness: Meditation provides an opportunity to observe the internal dialogue and impulses that lead to procrastination. Is it a desire for instant gratification? A feeling of inadequacy? By becoming aware of these patterns without judgment, one can begin to disengage from them.

Cultivating Inner Peace: The hurried, anxious energy that often accompanies procrastination can be calmed through meditation. A peaceful mind is more conducive to focused work and sustained effort.

Rehearsing Productive Action: Through meditative visualization, one can mentally "rehearse" the steps needed to complete a task, making the actual execution feel less daunting and more familiar.

Integration for Holistic Overcoming of Procrastination

The true power lies in integrating these practices.

Start the day with scriptural mindfulness, reading a passage that inspires diligence and purpose, meditating on its meaning.

Follow with prayer, asking for strength, focus, and wisdom for the tasks ahead, specifically addressing any known procrastination tendencies.

Throughout the day, when the urge to procrastinate arises, pause for a moment of meditation, perhaps a few mindful breaths, to regain presence and reconnect with the intention set earlier. Recalling a key scripture during this time can reinforce the commitment.

Before starting a difficult task, take a few moments for focused meditation to visualize success and affirm one's capabilities, perhaps accompanied by a short prayer for guidance.

By consistently applying scriptural mindfulness, prayer, and meditation, individuals can develop a robust internal framework that systematically addresses the psychological, emotional, and spiritual roots of procrastination, leading to greater productivity, peace, and fulfillment.

Procrastination can be a challenging habit to break, but the Bible offers numerous principles and promises that can encourage diligence, wisdom, and purposeful action. Here's a list of scriptures and corresponding affirmations to help overcome procrastination:

Bible Scriptures and Affirmations to Overcome Procrastination

Diligence and Hard Work

Proverbs 10:4: "Lazy hands make for poverty, but diligent hands bring wealth."

Affirmation: "I am diligent and hardworking. My efforts bring forth abundance and blessing."

Proverbs 13:4: "The soul of the sluggard craves and gets nothing, while the soul of the diligent is richly supplied."

Affirmation: "I am a diligent worker, and I will be richly supplied. My desires are met through consistent action."

Proverbs 14:23: "In all toil there is profit, but mere talk tends only to poverty."

Affirmation: "My labor is profitable. I choose action over idle talk, and my work yields good returns."

Proverbs 21:5: "The plans of the diligent lead surely to abundance, but everyone who is hasty comes only to poverty."

Affirmation: "My diligent plans lead to abundance. I am focused and purposeful in my efforts."

Romans 12:11: "Never be lacking in zeal, but keep your spiritual fervor, serving the Lord."

Affirmation: "I am zealous and fervent in spirit. I serve with enthusiasm and purpose, honoring God in all I do."

Making the Most of Time

Ecclesiastes 9:10a: "Whatever your hand finds to do, do it with your might..."

Affirmation: "I do everything with all my might. I embrace each task with strength and dedication."

Ephesians 5:15-16: "Look carefully then how you walk, not as unwise but as wise, making the best use of the time, because the days are evil."

Affirmation: "I am wise and intentional with my time. I make the most of every opportunity, redeeming the days."

John 9:4: "We must work the works of him who sent me while it is day; night is coming, when no one can work."

Affirmation: "I work diligently while it is day, understanding the urgency of the present moment. I seize opportunities to accomplish what is needed."

Overcoming Excuses and Fear

Proverbs 26:13: "The sluggard says, 'There is a lion in the road! There is a lion in the streets!'"

Affirmation: "I refuse to make excuses. I face challenges head-on and move forward with courage."

Philippians 4:13: "I can do all things through Christ who strengthens me."

Affirmation: "I am strong and capable through Christ. I can overcome any obstacle, including procrastination, with His help."

Taking Action and Completing Tasks

Colossians 3:23-24: "Whatever you do, work heartily, as for the Lord and not for men, knowing that from the Lord you will receive the inheritance as your reward. You are serving the Lord Christ."

Affirmation: "I work heartily, as unto the Lord. Every task I complete is an act of service and brings me closer to my reward."

James 4:17: "So whoever knows the right thing to do and fails to do it, for him it is sin."

Affirmation: "I act on what I know is right. I choose obedience and follow through on my responsibilities."

Galatians 6:9: "And let us not grow weary of doing good, for in due season we will reap, if we do not give up."

Affirmation: "I will not grow weary in doing good. I persist in my efforts, knowing that a harvest of blessings awaits me when I do not give up."

Planning and Order

1 Corinthians 14:40: "But all things should be done decently and in order."

Affirmation: "I bring order and decency to my tasks. I plan effectively and execute systematically."

Proverbs 16:3: "Commit your work to the Lord, and your plans will be established."

Affirmation: "I commit my work and plans to the Lord. He establishes my steps, and I move forward with divine guidance."

By meditating on these scriptures and consistently affirming their truths, you can rewire your thought patterns and cultivate habits of diligence, purpose, and effective action.

Overcoming procrastination yields numerous benefits, primarily fostering a sense of control and peace of mind. By tackling tasks promptly, individuals experience reduced stress and anxiety often associated with looming deadlines, leading to improved mental well-being. This proactive approach boosts productivity and efficiency, as tasks are completed without the hurried, often lower-quality, output of last-minute efforts. Moreover, conquering procrastination enhances self-confidence and a feeling of competence, replacing the helplessness that often accompanies chronic delay with a sense of strength and purpose. Ultimately, it allows for better time management, increased personal freedom, and a clearer path towards achieving goals.

Congratulations on taking the initiative to implement strategies to overcome procrastination; your dedication to self-improvement is commendable and will undoubtedly lead to greater success and peace of mind. You can overcome procrastination!

www.ingramcontent.com/pod-product-compliance
Lightning Source LLC
Chambersburg PA
CBHW051321120626
46547CB00015B/2342